THE

mizz®

GUIDE TO BOYS!

Text copyright © Panini UK Ltd 2010
Illustrations: Joanna Baldock. Copyright © Panini UK Ltd 2010
Cover photography: Shutterstock

With special thanks to:
Joanna Baldock, Lisa Clark, Kate Miller
and Karen O'Brien

Published in Great Britain in 2010
by Panini Books

A catalogue record of this book is available from the British Library.

ISBN: 978-1-84653-115-6

Printed and bound in England by Clays Ltd, St Ives plc

Panini Books a division of Panini UK Ltd.
Brockbourne House, 77 Mount Ephraim, Tunbridge Wells, Kent, TN4 8BS

Virgin Pulp used during manufacture of the paper has been sourced
from sustainably managed forests certified by the Pan European Forest
Certification (PEFC) organisation.

CONTENTS

INTRODUCTION

Boys don't have to be a mystery. We've got the straight scoop on all your most pressing questions so you can finally figure out what he's really thinking.

The *Mizz* Guide to Boys is filled with everything you need to banish boy drama, understand lad behaviour, bust boy myths and maybe even lip-lock with boykind!

CHAPTER ONE
BOYS: DECODED
The meaning of boy!

BODY LANGUAGE BASICS

What a boy says only tells half the story. Match up these common male moves and discover how well you can decode his hidden hints.

BEHAVIOUR

1. Puts you in a head lock
2. Wraps his arm around your waist
3. Mimics your moves
4. Stands with his arms crossed
5. Pokes you in the ribs

MEANINGS

A. He's totally in tune with you
B. Immature or not, he's trying to tell you that he likes you!
C. Warning! This boy is either a super-grouch or he's signalling for you to stay away
D. He's got you pegged as kid sister territory
E. He feels protective of you

ANSWERS: 1. D; 2. E; 3. A; 4. C; 5. B

SCORING

Count how many you got correct, then check out how well you know boys...

5 – Way to go! You're a whizz at picking up on boy clues. Read on to see what else you can add to your boy-clopedia of knowledge.

3 to 4 – You've got the basics, but once you learn how to recognise his subtle signals, you'll be laughing!

0 to 2 – Looks like a little guidance is needed. Get comfy and keep reading. You'll have it down in no time.

EVER WONDERED WHY BOYS...

Feel the need to prove they're oh-so strong?

From video game antics to rough sports or laughing instead of crying at a sad movie, boys seem to be conditioned to be physically and emotionally tough as nails. Truth is, society still looks to traditional stereotypes to determine how guys and girls act, which means the boys think they've got to play Mr. Tough Guy. What's a girl to do? Chances are he's not going to dish his feelings to you, but if he does, be sure to listen up.

Ask for your number, but never rings?

You've got to admit that it takes guts for a boy to ask for your number, and even more courage to actually call. From his point of view, calling a girl means putting himself out there and potentially getting rejected. Ouch, right? He doesn't want to seem too desperate or too eager, so ease his nerves by supplying a little positive reinforcement when the guy asks or (gasp!) calls.

Pay zero attention to you in front of their friends?

So, that hottie never has a problem chatting you up when he's flying solo, but the second his friends whip around the corner, you're nonexistent. This Jekyll and Hyde routine could come from his need to make sure his pals feel like they're his top priority. Just like some girls feel threatened when a new girl comes into your group, a boy's friends worry they'll lose their bud to you. Play it cool with his pals and be friendly so they know they aren't competing with you for his time.

Remember every sports stat, but go blank on what you said five seconds ago?

It's all about focus. Boys aren't trained to be natural listeners the way girls are. A guy might actually be interested in what you're saying, but because he probably can't boast about your new outfit to his friends, he's likely to tune it out. Try meeting him halfway and chat about something in neutral territory, like movies or music. But you also have to remember that boys are very different to girls in this area and make allowances for them!

Never seem to get your hints?

Want him to ask you out? Or help you with a difficult assignment? Don't bother being subtle because most boys simply aren't wired to pick up on sly clues. They're used to speaking with one another in a very straightforward language, so what girls consider the most obvious hint is actually an unintelligible code to them. Do yourself a favour – tell him how you feel, explain exactly why you're upset and spell out what you mean, it'll save you both loads of frustration.

BOY SPEAK BUSTED!

Is he for real or a timewaster? Why's he taking so long to reply? Find the hidden truths behind his messages...

A text is often a boy's first move towards getting to know you. So, what he says and how he says it is key...

> ## "Hi gorgeous!"
> ## (Or hon, babe, sweetie...)

He's a charmer! The first few messages are a chance to test the water. Being overfriendly verging on a smarmy may show arrogance. He's skipped the "Getting to know you" stage – bad move. Is he a player? More than likely!

> ## "Hey, how's it goin'?"

He's keeping it casual, but he's taking an interest. Our advice? Play it cool back, but be friendly so he knows you're interested. Make sure you ask him some questions to keep the conversation flowing.

> ## "Got your number from _____ hope u don't mind?!"

To go to the effort of getting your number from someone else means he's either a bit of a stalker (doubtful), or really into you. If you like him back, great! If not, be honest with him. Don't drag it out – that's just cruel. Think of it like pulling off a plaster – done quickly it may sting, but it won't hurt for too long!

"XXXXXX"

Kisses. Don't stress over how many he puts on the end. Some is better than none, but a lot of people just aren't text kissers. The fact he's messaging you in the first place probably shows he likes you, so why fret over a few little crosses?

"Gotta go/talk soon/see you around"

This one's a toughie. Is he fobbing you off or does he really have to be somewhere? If he ends the chat abruptly, doesn't answer your questions or cuts you off mid-flow, the likelihood is he's keen to get rid of you. If you're not sure, wait. If he's busy he'll text you when he's free. If not, you've got your answer. Don't start texting him to find out why he's not replying. Just leave it and move on.

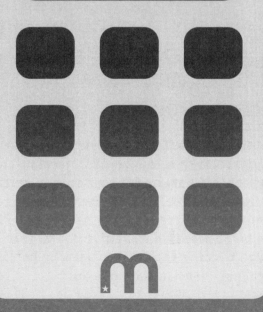

THE WAITING GAME

How soon is too soon and late is too late for him to reply to your text? There's a fine line between playing hard to get and being rude, and that applies to you, too...

1 MINUTE

Too keen, maybe? Either he's a mobile phone addict with no other social life to speak of, or he's verging on the obsessive.

30 MINS-1 HOUR

He's not keeping you waiting but he isn't so quick to get back to you that he seems desperate. It's a good sign.

2-3 HOURS

Treat 'em mean, keep 'em keen. Either he's busy or he's a game player. If he often does this, it's probably the latter. (Think about where he is though — is he at footie practice or having his tea?

THE NEXT DAY

24hrs and he couldn't even spare half a minute to reply? Alarm bells!

LONGER THAN A DAY

We hate to say it, but he's probably not that interested or bothered. He got your text and ignored it, then forgot about it pretty much instantly. Then, a few days later, while he was bored on a bus and clearing his in-box, he found it again and sent you a token reply to be polite. Ouch!

BUT ASK YOURSELF THIS...

How regularly do you text him? If you keep him in suspense, he may be seeing if you like a taste of your own medicine! What are his replies like? If they're a bit frosty or offish, try not to hold out too much hope.

Boy Secrets

Ever wondered what boys are thinking? Here are 5 things they wish you knew...

1 A LITTLE MYSTERY IS A GOOD THING

Ever notice how boys don't talk a lot, especially when it comes to talking about themselves? They don't feel like it's totally necessary for everyone to know everything, like what they ate for lunch or who they texted. And maybe they don't want to know every tiny thing about you. Instead of talking about yourself all the time, try waiting until he asks a question. He will, we promise.

2 CLOTHES ARE NOT THE MOST IMPORTANT THING IN THE WORLD

Ever seen a lad burst into tears because his best friend is wearing the same shirt? Or, because he can't get a hoodie in the right shade of blue? Never! They just don't function that way. You've got to realise life won't come to a crashing halt if you and another girl at school are both wearing the same skirt...or jumper...or shoes...or whatever.

3 YOU CAN'T READ MINDS

If a boyf wants to know how you're feeling, he'll usually ask. Girls think they have a 'sixth sense' about lads, so they read into everything: if he's quiet, it means he doesn't like you; If he looks at another girl, you're about to get dumped; If he doesn't email you back right away, it's over. Right? Wrong. Calm down, take a deep breath and if you still just have to know what's going on in his head, ask him.

4 IF YOU'RE HUNGRY YOU SHOULD EAT

When a boy is hungry, he says, "I'm starvin'," then he eats – the end. Boys typically think it's lame when girls talk about food/diets/calories all the time. It gets really old, really fast. They also appreciate a girl who eats normally – that means no starving herself and no obsessing endlessly over the size of her thighs. Honestly, they just don't get that. So eat lunch and stop talking about it. Not only will boykind be grateful, you'll also quit focusing negative energy on your body image and you'll be feeling more positive and confident too – hurrah!

5 SECRETS ARE SACRED

Despite what you might think, boys don't really gossip, especially about girls. They might tell a close friend they're crushing on a girl, but guys don't usually get chatty and spread rumours. When a boy does tell his best bud a secret, he knows it won't be all over school by the end of the day. Lads know how to keep info on the down-low and you should too.

BOY BODY LANGUAGE

Not sure if a lad fancies you or whether he's just being friendly? Here's how to spot the signs that give him away when he wants to be more than good mates...

WHEN YOU SEE HIM

He may not say a word, but his body language will speak his true feelings loud and clear! This consists of the little movements that people make, usually without realising it, and is a part of how we communicate. Small things – like the way he stands, the gestures he makes and how he acts in general around you – will signal whether or not he's interested in you.

So, which signs should you watch out for? Well, people who fancy each other often move 'in sync'. This isn't to say you'll do the exact same thing at the precise second, but he may 'mirror' you – if you sip your drink, he'll grab his glass a split-second later. Or if you scratch your nose, he might too!

He may also stand with his hands on his hips – this is meant to show off his big, strong bod and his confidence in it! Or he'll angle his body towards you, too, leaning in when he speaks or having his feet pointing at you even if he's talking to someone else. This is a signal he wants to get closer.

WHEN YOU TALK TO HIM

It's not what he says but how he says it. Facial expressions, gestures and how he puts things can reveal his thoughts!

If you catch him looking at you as you talk, and he smiles when your eyes meet, there's a good chance he fancies you! The more he does this, the more he likes you. If he can't take his eyes off you or his pupils get larger, it's a sure sign he's attracted to you!

This one is a conversational thing, but as it's subconscious, not deliberate, it still counts! If you've spoken to him before, he may mention details from your last chat or use phrases he's picked up from you. This is a sign that you've got his attention and that he listens to what you say.

He might tease you! Some lads don't know how to express themselves that well, so he may diss your celeb crush or make a smart remark about your new 'do. It's not a smooth chat-up, but he's not doing it to be nasty, just to show you he's noticed you. Be friendly and tease him back – then, as his confidence grows, he may start to communicate like a mature human being!

Remember, some lads are just shy! Signs of nerves include tucking his head into his shoulders like he's trying to make himself invisible. He may also avoid eye contact and look embarrassed or flustered whenever you're around. Just smile and be friendly and may eventually coax him out of his shell.

If he likes you he might...

☑ ASK HIS FRIENDS TO TALK TO YOU
If one of his mates strikes up a convo with you out of the blue, it's probably because he's been asked to find out if you're interested. Whatever you tell his pals will be passed on to him – so drop hints that you like him and don't say anything bad! However, if he wants a date he should ask you himself, not get his friends to fix it up.

☑ GET TALKING TO YOUR GANG
If this happens, don't automatically assume he fancies one of them rather than you! He may just be sounding them out to see if you like him, or getting inside info like what kind of music and hobbies you're into.

☑ ACT UP SO YOU'LL NOTICE HIM
You know how your five-year-old bro shows off for attention? Well, older boys are just the same! If he

starts clowning around or gets really loud or laddish, he's trying to get you to notice him, letting you know he's into you without actually saying so. Also, over-the-top movements, like arm-waving or silly walks are a sign he wants to stand out. Lame, but go easy on him – he'll calm down as he gets more comfy around you.

☑ DO NICE THINGS FOR YOU

If he offers to carry your school books, holds the door open for you or offers you his seat on the bus, it's pretty obvious he wants to be in your good books! Most lads only use this tactic as a very last resort, though, as it's guaranteed to make them feel a bit daft in front of their friends!

Even though these signals can show a lad likes you, they're not absolute proof. The only way to know for sure is if he tells you! So, instead of waiting for him to give you a sign, why not be brave and ask him out?

CHAPTER TWO
FLIRTING SECRETS
Bag that boy!

WHAT'S YOUR MOVE?

So you have a huge crush on that hot boy in Maths class. What's your move? Do you wait around for him to whisk you away or are you more into sweeping him off his feet?

Your favourite part of PE is...
A Asking the buff boys to show you their techniques ❏
for push ups.
B Wowing your current cutie with your netball serve. ❏
C Catching a glimpse of your crush playing football. ❏

You're at your local shopping centre with your BFF when you spot some good-looking boys. When it's obvious the lads are focusing on her, you...
A Announce that you're feeling a little light-headed ❏
and ask the cutest boy in the bunch to get some air.
How could he resist?
B Ask the guy in the football shirt what he thought ❏
of Saturday's game. Maybe he'll appreciate your
sporty knowledge.
C Say you're scooting into New Look to check out a ❏
dress on sale.

You're bored in art class and find yourself doodling around your notes. What do you draw?
A "I heart" and then the first name of your favourite ❏
five boys.
B Your first name paired with your current crush's ❏
last name in loopy writing.

C The secret nickname you have for your crush, ❏
but then you cross it out so no one will see if they
glance at your notes.

You're at the school disco when your crush shows up with – gasp! – another girl. How do you deal?

A Ask your crush if you can cut in for a slow dance, ❏
It's not like she's his GF.

B Ask all your boy mates to dance with you to make ❏
him jealous…all the while flashing flirty smiles at
your crush.

C Sigh. You made such an effort too, so you throw ❏
him a few of your fabbest smiles in the hope he'll
notice you.

You can't get the guy from your geography class to even glance your way. How do you plan on finally getting his attention?

A Fail your 'Name the 50 states of America' test ❏
on purpose so that you can ask him for an after-
school study session. Ummm… Alaska is is in the
Midwest, right?

B Stop him in the corridor and fake that you forgot ❏
to copy down the homework so the two of you can
start talking.

C Stare in his general direction for the entire 40 ❏
minutes of class. If anyone asks, you're studying the
map behind him.

Now check your scores on the next page!

HUSHED HUNNIE
From meaningful glances to sly smiles, you've got the right moves – it's just that they're a little, well…quiet. So it's time to turn it up a notch. If you're super shy, take it slow – a quick 'hey, how are you?' in the corridor will go a long way.

MOSTLY B'S

FAB FLIRTER
Congrats! Your advances are awesomely on target. You're smart about showing an interest by staying relaxed, confident and just being yourself. Your casual-but-cool 'tude makes boys notice you right away. Keep it up and you'll find a top boyf!

MOSTLY C'S

MAN-EATER
High fives for having the guts to go after the boy. But be warned: some of your crush-catching moves might be a little over the top. Take a chance on the one cutie you're really crazy about by trying tamer tactics – a simple smile should do the trick!

Boys – The crush chart

What's your type? Check out our crush chart to see which kind of lad you go for – and where to find him!

HANGOUT:
school library

FAVOURITE ACCESSORY:
book

HE'D MAKE A GOOD BOYFRIEND BECAUSE:
he'd honestly want to hear about your feelings

ANNOYING HABIT:
sketching your portrait during lessons

CHAT UP LINE:
"Would you like to get an expresso?"

DREAM JOB:
English professor

Bad Boy

HANGOUT:
the park

FAVOURITE ACCESSORY:
chain wallet

HE'D MAKE A GOOD BOYFRIEND BECAUSE:
you could take him home to make your parents mad

ANNOYING HABIT:
pretending he's cooler than everyone else

CHAT UP LINE:
"Check out my new tattoo."

DREAM JOB:
what job?

HANGOUT:
his home studio

FAVOURITE
ACCESSORY:
new trainers

HE'D MAKE A
GOOD BOYFRIEND
BECAUSE:
he'd be your
"soldier"

ANNOYING HABIT:
calling you
his "boo"

CHAT UP LINE:
"Let's kick it
later, shorty"

DREAM JOB:
taking over
from JayZ

*Hip-hop
hottie*

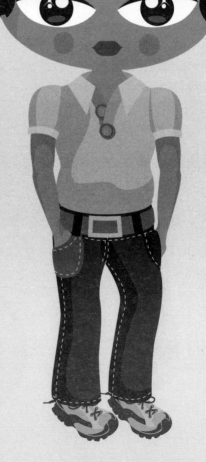

Sporty Type

HANGOUT:
the school gym

FAVOURITE
ACCESSORY:
a baseball cap

HE'D MAKE A
GOOD BOYFRIEND
BECAUSE:
**he's a sure thing
for prom king**

ANNOYING HABIT:
**watching sports
24/7**

CHAT UP LINE:
**"Meet me outside
the gym after the
game."**

DREAM JOB:
**professional
footballer**

Mr. Smarty Pants

HANGOUT:
the science lab

FAVOURITE ACCESSORY:
laptop

HE'D MAKE A GOOD
BOYFRIEND BECAUSE:
**he'd help with your
homework**

ANNOYING HABIT:
**always knowing
the answers**

CHAT UP LINE:
**"How about joining
my after-school
study class?"**

DREAM JOB:
medical researcher

28

DISCOVER YOUR FLIRT STYLE

1. The guy you fancy gets the same bus as you to school. Every morning you:

a. Smile as you walk on past

b. Quitely say hi and go back to reading

c. Shout 'awright' then go chat to another cute boy

d. Sit next to him and ask him about himself

2. A gorgeous guy asks if you have plans for Friday night. You respond by…

a. Pretending you can't hear and rushing off

b. Oh, I might have a date.

c. Sassily saying 'Maybe I don't, why?"

d. By inviting him out to the movies

3. You're crushing on your bessie's bro. When you go to her house. You:

a. Giggle loudly as you make snacks in the kitchen

b. Hide in her room while she fetches a DVD

c. Invite him to hang out too

d. Head directly to his room to say hi

4. You're at a party and everyone from your class is there, including the hottie. You:

a. Mingle with everyone but ignore him on purpose

b. Smile, then disappear into another room so he can't see you blush

c. Get all your mates laughing and playing games

d. Go over and see if he wants to dance

5. You receive a text from a cute boy. He's got your number from someone else. You:

a. Leave it for a couple of hours then text back "How's it goin?"

b. Ask all your mates what to do

c. Text back with a "Nick who? x"

d. Reply immediately asking him to meet at lunch break

A'S MYSTERIOUS MINX

It's all about mystery with you. You like to make boys wonder, "what's this girl all about?" Boys are attracted to you because they think it's cool you don't put it all out there. You're like a hot puzzle they have to solve.

COOL CUES

★ If he asks what you've been up to, tell him some details, but not everything. Keep him guessing.

★Play up the drama. A mischievous smile from across the room will totally intrigue him.

★Invite him to go to go rock climbing or another activity he'd never think of doing.

B'S COY CUTIE

You're a shy one. You tend to shrink from flirty behaviour, and leave it up to the boy to make the moves. That can be a good plan because lots of lads like taking the lead. Just make sure you're not being too bashful – let the boy know you like him.

MODEST MOVES

★ Smile when you see your crush and let your hand touch his arm when you talk so he gets the hint.

★ Hang out where he is – like if he's a lifeguard at the weekend, go to the pool with a group of friends.

★ Laugh at his jokes or say you think he has a nice smile – it'll give him confidence that you're into him.

C'S PLAYFUL PAL

You flirt by playing around with boys, kinda like a buddy but more like a buddy they might get to kiss! What makes your flirt style work is that one minute they're thinking how much fun you are, and then suddenly they're crushing on you.

FRIENDLY FLIRTS

★ When you hang out, casually put your arm around his shoulder or touch his leg when you sit together.
★ Joke around the way you do with your girl friends. If your pals think you're great, then he will, too!
★ Invite him to go out with you and your friends. Make it sound casual, but then see where things go.

D'S STRAIGHTFORWARD SWEETIE

The way you flirt is super-direct. You're not afraid to go after the boy or do all the typical things: You turn on the charm, amp up the physical contact, give him meaningful looks – a boy would have to be an idiot not to get it.

MORE MOVES

★ Compliment him. Lads love flattery. If you know he plays football. Say "I heard you are really good."
★ Are you a good listener? If you get him to open up and talk about himself, he might feel closer to you.
★ Make the first move, but then let him take the lead. Ask him out but then let him text you about your date.

31

GET HIS ATTENTION

Want your crush to fall for you? Follow these boy-snagging tips…

MAKE CONVERSATION

Talk to him about something personal or interesting, not boring topics, like school or homework. For example, if you approach your cutie at a swimming competition, tell him the funny story about how your parents had to bribe you with an ice cream sundae to jump off the high dive and by the time you finally jumped, the ice cream shop was closed. Stories like that have a way of making people want to share their experiences, too. Next thing you know, you've bonded!

STAY COOL

Remember that even though this guy is the star of your dreams, in real life he has fears and insecurities just like you. And you never know, he could be as nervous talking to you as you are talking to him! If you stay relaxed, so will he.

COMPLIMENT HIM

Everyone loves flattery. The trick: you have to mean what you say. If your crush is wearing a tee with a band logo, tell him you like it. Then ask what other music he listens to. If you thought he was awesome in the school play, let him know. Then ask if he wants help with

running through his lines before the next performance. Be cool and be genuine. If you don't mean it your fakeness will be obvious and you may frighten him off!

SEND HIM SIGNALS

Use subtle body language to give him the hint that you're crushing. When you pass him in the hallway, smile and hold his gaze for a few seconds before looking away. When you talk to him, maybe touch his arm when he says something amusing. Physical contact will give him a chance to get the hint that you really like him. But if he moves away or resists, he's sending the signal that he's not interested. In that case, don't invade his space and back off a bit.

DOES HE REALLY LIKE YOU?

If you can't tell already, take this quiz and find out for sure!

How often do you see your crush?
A. Once in a while in the corridor between classes
B. Pretty often, but you hardly ever hang together because you don't really have any friends in common
C. All the time – you've been friends for ages

You've just got braces and you're feeling very self-conscious about them. Your crush:
A. Doesn't mention them at all
B. Laughs and makes a 'metal mouth' joke
C. Says, "You still look nice!"

If you miss more than one day at school, your crush:
A. Seems like he didn't even know you were away
B. Texts and asks, "Do you want to borrow my notes?"
C. Asks about where you've been

You're in the school cafeteria when you spill orange juice all down your white shirt. Your crush:
A. Walks right past without saying a word
B. Laughs along with his gang
C. Hands you his napkin

Your dream guy just biked past your house. When you yell hi, he:
A. Just keeps pedalling
B. Grins and asks what you're doing
C. Turns red and says, "Uh, I didn't know you lived here."

MOSTLY AS
He's just not for you

Finding out your crush isn't interested in you is harsh. Maybe he just doesn't know you well enough (yet!) to like you. Ask yourself if he's really worth a ton of effort. After all, there are so many crushworthy boys out there, why would you want to be with one who doesn't think you're absolutely, positively amazing? Stop spending your energy on a guy who's not paying attention and keep your eyes open for the lad who is.

MOSTLY BS
He's sorta into you

Boys can be so hard to read – one minute they're making fun of you, the next they're being really sweet and then they act like you don't even exist! That unpredictable vibe is what's going on with your crush. He doesn't mean to confuse you, he just isn't sure how he feels about you. Let him get to know you better by hanging out together with other friends. If he doesn't figure out how he feels about you soon, then it's time to move on.

MOSTLY CS
He totally likes you

True, we can't read minds, but all the signs point to this boy being completely into you. So now what? Let him know you like him, too! Forget about any drastic measures, like a long, emotional letter or pressure from your friends – he most likely will freak a bit if you suddenly come on too strong. Instead, give him your best smile every time you see him, chat with him about his weekend plans and let him know you hope to hang out with him soon!

FLIRTOLOGY

He's cute, so how can you catch his attention – and keep it? It's actually easier than you think…

Some animals, like baboons, have an upfront approach to romance. When a female sees a male she fancies, she flashes her bum in his face, then grabs his hand and marches him off into the jungle. Unless you want to risk terrifying your crush – and earning yourself a rep as a very weird girl in the process – you probably need to be more subtle than that. So here's how to give him all the right signals – they're virtually guaranteed to make him notice you, even if he's not quite sure why at first…

PEEK-A-BOO
Flirting expert Pamela Johnson suggests the 'look and look away' manoeuvre – think of it as a more grown-up game of peek-a-boo. Glance at your crush's eyes and then look away. Wait a second or two, then steal another glance, before looking down. A couple of seconds later, look at him again. He won't be able to stop staring at you!

PROP UP

Don't waste hours agonising over how to dress to impress him. Instead, pick a 'prop' – one striking item that'll grab his attention and give him something to chat to you about. It could be a neclklace, belt or cool band tour shirt. Just make sure you're suitably clued up. If you're wearing a Klaxons tee but can't name any of their songs, it could get cringey!

SAY HELLO

Relationships guru Tracey Cox says the more you interact with someone, the more they'll like you, so don't play cool or hard to get. Say hi and stop to chat every now and again. Lads like outgoing, confident girls.

SMILE PLEASE!

Smiling is contagious and will make you seem friendly and approachable – as long as it's genuine, not forced. It lights up your face and draws people to you. Boys tend to be attracted to smiling, happy girls who look like they're having fun! This can work even if you are painfully shy.

How not to do it...

💜 Don't freeze in fear – people might mistake you for a coat stand and start to hang their jackets on you!

💜 Clutching onto your bag so hard that your fingers go white, fiddling with things or obsessively flattening down your hair may look a bit strange and neurotic.

💜 Biting your nails while someone's talking to you is plain rude. And a bit gross.

Flirting do's & don'ts

Want to stay cool around your crush? Follow these hints for foolproof flirting...

 DO
Make your boyfriend his favourite ice-cream sundae

 DON'T
Bring it to him while he and his mates are practising BMX tricks

 DO
Flirt with the hottie working in your fave café.

 DON'T
Forget to find out if he has a girlfriend first!

 DO
Show up at the beach when you know your crush is going to be there

DON'T
Ask your best friend's boyfriend to rub sun tan lotion on your back

 DO
Ask your crush to give up a day with his buds to hang with you

 DON'T
Demand your guy spends every free second with you and only you

 DO
Surprise your boyfriend with concert tickets

 DON'T
Get tickets for The Saturdays or Girls Aloud when you know he'd hate it

 DO
Expect romance to come your way

 DON'T
Be disappointed if you haven't met your dream boy just yet

CHAPTER THREE
THE DEAL ON DATING
Take the plunge!

ASK HIM OUT (THE RIGHT WAY!)

Unless you know he's completely into you, asking a boy out can be scary. What if he says no or just laughs in your face? Ouch! Taking a chance isn't easy, but being brave could be really worth it. Before you make your move, check out our plan to get your dream-date dude.

IF HE'S A FRIEND

You hang out with this boy on a regular basis, you have a lot of the same friends and may even talk on the phone or IM, but he has no idea you're crushin' on him.

SET IT UP
Start giving this boy some extra attention. When you're all hanging out, make it a point to be near him. If you're sitting at a table, take the seat across from him so you can give him a flirty smile. Casually touch his arm while you're talking or give him a friendly little nudge in the hallway between classes (but don't overdo it).

MAKE YOUR MOVE
The next time your crowd is at the movies, ask him to help you with the popcorn and fizzy drinks. Once you're one-on-one with the boy, say something to let him know you've been noticing him like, "Hey, that was a great speech you gave in class" or "I like your new jacket."

ASK THE QUESTION
Call him when you know he won't be busy. Asking over the phone can give you a bit more courage because you're not face-to-face. If no one answers, don't leave a message – waiting for him to call back is unnecessary torture. When you do get him on the phone, ask him to do something specific that you're both interested in like, "I'm on my way to the skate park, wanna come?" If he starts acting weird, mention that some of your friends will be there and it's no big deal if he can't make it. Then call some pals and head to the park (if he shows up, you won't be a liar!) Yeah, you'll be bummed if he bails this time, but if he says yes, you've got yourself a date!

IF YOU KINDA KNOW HIM

You see him at school and at parties, but you've only spoken to him once or twice, if at all.

SET IT UP

Start by finding out what you and this boy have in common. What do your buds know about him? What kind of music does he listen to? Do people think he's as cool as he is cute? No need to waste your time if he's just a hot jerk. But be sure to keep a low profile – don't ask a million questions. You don't want everyone else to know you're interested, right? If there's a mutual interest, like you're both really into the same band, you're already half way there!

MAKE YOUR MOVE

You hear he'll be at the big party Friday night. Make plans for you and your girls to be at the party too. (Remember, you don't really know this boy. What if he's a lame-o? You'll need someone else to talk to.) After a while, tear yourself away from the group and casually bump into him or strike up a conversation using the info you dug up like, "I heard you sometimes DJ. How'd you get into that?"

ASK THE QUESTION

At school, pick up where you left off. Catch him chilling with his MP3 player, tap him on the shoulder and say, "Remember me from the party?" Then flash him a smile and add, "Want to check out the battle of the bands this weekend?" If he says he has other plans but keeps chatting, it means he's at least interested, so don't totally write him off. If he says no, simply reply, "Too bad. I hear it's going to be a rockin' show," and walk away with your ego intact!

IF YOU DON'T KNOW HIS NAME

You spotted him at the movies or the football match, but he must go to another school because you have no idea who he is. In a weird way, this is actually the easiest scenario because you can totally avoid him if things don't work out.

SET IT UP

You have to make sure he notices you. If you're with pals, enjoy yourself – laugh, tell stories and be sure to glance at him once in a while. Don't stare, though, because you don't want to scare the boy! He'll probably look at you – good vibes attract people. When he glances your way, hold his gaze for two or three seconds, then look away. Or grab a friend and walk by him (it may sound corny, but to be successful, he has to see you).

MAKE YOUR MOVE

You never know when you're going to have a chance with this cutie again, so you have to act fast. If you're at the movies, sit behind him. If you're at the music store, browse through the CD stack next to him. Break the ice with a question that requires more than a one-word answer like, "What do you think of this?" If he responds, ask him something about himself like, "Where do you go to school?"

ASK THE QUESTION

Tell him about a flick you're planning to see and ask if he's interested in going, too. Get his email address, then send him the deets and make sure he's still up for the movie. If so, meet him at the cinema, but with a group of your mates – always meet someone new in a public place just to be safe. If he says no, at least you tried – good for you, girl!

WHAT'S YOUR PERFECT DATE?

If you could go anywhere in the world right now, where would it be?

A. Paris – so romantic…

B. Germany – for the cool music festivals

C. Australia – sun, sea, sand, surf…and surfers!

You're off to the cinema. Which kind of film would you like to watch?

A. A romantic comedy or maybe even a tear-jerker

B. A blood-chilling horror

C. A Harry Potter-style fantasy

Gangs of friends are often made up of different types of girls. Which one are you?

A. The sweet girlie-girl

B. Miss Cool

C. The joker

If you could choose the perfect gift from your crush, what would it be?

A. A huge bunch of flowers and a box of chocolates

B. A lovingly compiled mix CD

C. I don't know, surprise me!

Which lesson do you most enjoy at school?

A. English lit or history – you love to read about more decadent times

B. Music – especially when you get to play it

C. Geography – you want to see the world!

MOSTLY A'S

YOUR PERFECT DATE IS... *A romantic night in*

Aww…You're a soppy, slushy, romantic kind of gal who loves to be treated like a princess. A night in watching a rom-com is your perfect date, and if there's finger food, like popcorn, Maltesers or mini pizzas for you to feed each other – it would be bliss!

MOSTLY B'S

YOUR PERFECT DATE IS... *A gig*

Rocking out to cool bands is your idea of a kicking night out. You like to spend quality time with your lad – obviously – and enjoy a sesh of smooching as much as any gal. But you know there's much more to dating than kissing, so find yourself another music fan – a boy who'll understand just how alive a loud guitar can make you feel!

MOSTLY C'S

YOUR PERFECT DATE IS... *A theme park*

You have an outrageous, adventurous streak, and love adrenaline-charged moments. Your ideal boy will be fun-loving with a brilliant sense of humour, and daring enough to join you on the scariest, most stomach-churning rides. Laughing and screaming together will help you to bond, and you'll also have the perfect excuse to snuggle up to him – it may distract him from how scared he is!

GETTING PARENTAL PERMISSION

Your parents say 'you're not dating until you're 18'. How do you get them on side? Read on...

✓ Ask your parents what a 'date' means to them. Chances are, it's you + boy + alone = no. To ease their worries, add some parent-approved people to the equation by having a bunch of friends over to your place along with your crush. Keep it on the just-hanging-out level until your folks feel better about the situation.

✓ Take baby steps. Once mum and dad know your boyf, it's time to say, "Can I invite him over to watch a DVD?" After a few one-to-one visits and everyone is comfy, see if you two can catch a flick at the cinema. If they insist on driving say, "Sure, thanks!" Fight one battle at a time!

PSYCH YOURSELF UP

 Your crush is on his way over. Don't just run around your room freaking out, try to chill.

 Put on your fave music. It'll help to take your mind off the date and feel more confident.

✓ Dress in your cutest outfit. Avoid trying something new because you want to be comfy and secure with how you look. Wear what your best friends always say looks awesome on you. So what if he's already seen you in it? Boys never remember that stuff.

 Breathe deeply. Oh wait, was that the doorbell?

ANATOMY OF A DATE

Should you go out with him one-on-one, on a double date or get a whole group together? It depends…

ONE-ON-ONE
Why it's good: You can talk without being interrupted and learn more about each other. No one will be looking at you and there won't be any pressure for either of you to impress your pals.
Watch out for: Lulls in the conversation. Sometimes it just goes silent and you're like, "Errr…" Don't let this be you!

DOUBLE DATE
Why it's good: If the convo between you and your date dies, the other people can pick up the slack. Because there are only four of you, though, you won't have to fight for his attention.
Watch out for: The guys talking to each other and the girls having a girl-talk. You're supposed to be on a date with each other.

GROUP DATE
Why it's good: You don't have to worry so much about clicking with him when there are lots of people around. You can relax and just hang out.
Watch out for: Distractions. Don't let another girl chat his ear off. Get in at least one solid conversation with him.

DATING DISASTERS

How to deal when things don't go quite as, uh, planned.

DISASTER!

You have nothing to talk about

DATE SAVER: Just remember FAMIS: Friends and Family, Activities, Music/Movies, Interests, School. What do you and your friends do on the weekend? Do you have siblings? Are you in any clubs? Have you seen a really cool movie recently? Use the questions to get you both talking, but don't go overboard – after all, it's a friendly chat, not an interrogation!

DISASTER!

Your parents play chaperone

DATE SAVER: First, don't overreact. They aren't going to totally ruin your date. If dad's driving, ask if he can drop you off and come back later, or to give you both some space.

DISASTER!

You say something you wish you hadn't

DATE SAVER: So you're not a dog person and you say, "I hate dogs." Then he tells you he's had a dog for years and he loves them. Just correct your statement by saying, "Sorry if I offended you. I guess it's because I didn't grow up with dogs." Then leave it. Don't spend the next 15 minutes apologising or worrying. He probably won't even think about it for more than three seconds. More likely he's worrying about what he'll say next.

DISASTER!

You get food in your teeth or spill food all over yourself

DATE SAVER: If you notice spinach between your front teeth (or on your shirt), try not to panic. Seeing that you're not perfect might make him like you even better because he'll realise you're normal. Just pluck it out (or brush it off) and don't obsess. If you move on, so will he.

THE DEAL ON DATING

DATING FAQS

Settle your dating questions once and for all!

➜ *Who decides what to do or where to go on the date?*

When he asks what you want to do, don't say, "I don't know. What do you want to do?" You may think you're being polite, but you're really putting pressure on your cutie. He might stress out about whether you want to go to a party, movie or whatever. So help him out by having a few ideas in mind. It's not like you're dictating what you have to do, but you're giving some options you two can choose from together.

➜ *What shouldn't I talk about on a date?*

Hmm, maybe ex-boyfriends. Any mention of an ex will make your new boy feel like there's another guy on the date with you. Another taboo topic? Other girls. Don't put your crush on the spot by saying things like "Do you think that girl over there is pretty?" He doesn't know what answer you're fishing for, so don't trap him like that. Oh yeah, don't dig for compliments either. Of course he thinks you're gorgeous – he asked you out didn't he?

→ *Who should pay when you go out on a date?*

The best thing is to be ready to pay your share. Have your money out as you walk up to buy the movie tickets. Your date may let you, which is fine because it is the 21st century. Or, he may say, "No, I've got this." If you want to make sure knows you're not a moocher, say, "I'll buy the popcorn." That way you're telling him that you like being treated, but you don't need to be taken care of all the time thank-you very much!

So, how did the date go?

Here's a handy checklist to see if date No. 2 will happen!

 YOU BOTH LAUGHED ALL NIGHT LONG.

 YOU HAD LOTS TO TALK ABOUT.

 HE TOLD YOU PERSONAL STUFF.

 WHEN YOU TOLD STORIES, HE REALLY LISTENED AND ASKED QUESTIONS.

 HE DID SWEET THINGS LIKE HOLD DOORS OPEN FOR YOU.

 YOU FELT LIKE KISSING HIM, EVEN IF IT DIDN'T HAPPEN.

 YOUR INSTINCTS TELL YOU IT WENT WELL.

Scoring

5 TO 7 THUMBS UP
Wooohooo! It's time to get ready for your next fab date!

3 TO 5 THUMBS UP
Pretty good! Call him in a few days. If he sounds happy to hear from you, ask him if he'd like to meet you or catch a movie. If he sounds a little weirded out say, "Just wanted to say hi. See ya!" Now let him make the next move or you'll seem kind of desperate.

0 TO 2 THUMBS UP
Maybe you need a little more time to warm up to each other. Say hi when you see him. You might still get another chance with each other – only if you want to of course.

Write how your date went!

....
....
....
....
....
....
....
....
....
....
....
....
....
....
....
....
....
....
....
....
....
....

CHAPTER FOUR
SEALED WITH A KISS
Lip smacking tips!

TO KISS OR NOT TO KISS

It's the end of the night – the scary moment of truth! Should you lean in and kiss him? Will he smooch you? Think everyone kisses on the first date? No way! It's like a crazy urban legend that just won't go away. If the guy really likes you, he'll ask you out again. And if the date didn't go so well, kissing him definitely won't guarantee another one. And remember, don't kiss if you don't want to!

Stress-free snogging

Nervous? Don't be! With our tips, every kiss will be just like in the movies...

We've all been there – it's the end of the disco and you know your crush is about to move in for a lip-lock. Suddenly, your mind starts racing. Does your breath smell? Have you overdone the lip gloss? What if it goes wrong? Or will he just hate kissing you? You get yourself so worked up that, before you know it, you're muttering an excuse and scurrying off. Not so good...

DON'T PANIC!

EVERYONE GETS NERVOUS ABOUT KISSING, ESPECIALLY WHEN IT'S WITH SOMEONE NEW. IN FACT, WE BET EVEN ZAC EFRON GOT BUTTERFLIES THE FIRST TIME HE PUCKERED UP!

But how can you guarantee that your smooch sesh will be totally dreamy and hotter than a sunny summer afternoon? First read our guide, then just relax and get your snog on. After all, practise makes perfect!

BE PREPARED

If you reckon you're in for a bout of kissing, you need to be ready for it. Any snog will be a million times better if you feel relaxed, calm and confident – it's a scientifically proven fact. Well, kind of…

TRY THIS Chew some breath-freshening gum and slick on a thin layer of balm to keep your lips moist, but avoid wearing gloss or lippy, especially strong colours. Boys may like how it looks, but they won't want to end up wearing it after all the mouth-to-mouth action! And make sure you're alone. Snogging should be something private, not a spectator sport for all your mates.

SNOG SPOILER *Take out your gum before your lad's in sight – unless you want to him a surprise present mid-snog! Or just use a breath strip or spray to freshen up.*

> If you're not ready to kiss anyone, don't do it! Keep your kisses for someone special!

SPOTTING THE SIGNS

So, does he actually want to kiss you or not? Imagine how much you'll cringe if he moves in, you pucker up and it just turns out he wanted to whisper discreetly, as a mate, that you've got lippy on your teeth. You need to read his body language.

TRY THIS In the movie Hitch, 'date doctor' Will Smith advises, if a lad seems to be moving in on you, but you're not quite sure if he wants to a kiss, lean 20% of the way towards him. If he is working up to a snog, he should then take the hint and move in the other 80%. And if he's not, you won't look daft. Boys can be dumb or even shy – sometimes they need that final bit of encouragement.

SNOG SPOILER *You're going to feel pretty silly if you steam in for a lip-smaker and he pulls away in schock. So follow the 20/80 rule, and you'll be sure!*

A HAND-Y HINT

Where do you put your hands? It may sounds like a weird question, but you want to be enjoying your snog, not waving your mitts around awkwardly.

TRY THIS Some lads prefer them resting on their chest, their neck, face or back. Gently placing your hands on his chest or the front part of his shoulders can be good for controlling how hard he leans against you. Some lads get a bit carried away mid-snog, and may press forward so hard they push you off balance and you have to take a step back! Not a good look.

SNOG SPOILER *Don't lock your hands behind his neck. He might feel a bit trapped.*

POST-KISS ETIQUETTE

Don't yell "Wahey!" or text your mates about it in front of him. Not cool or classy!

TRY THIS Peck him on the mouth and keep eye-contact. If it was a good kiss, tell him – lads love an ego boost. But don't overdo it and appear too grateful!

SNOG SPOILER

Kisses may get a bit wet and slobbery, but try to resist wiping your face the second you stop snogging!

WHAT IF IT WAS A BAD KISS?

It's unlikely that you're going to stand there and say "Wow, that was horrible! I'm never doing that again!" but you may want to jokingly say something like, "Oh, I think we need a bit of practise!"

If you didn't enjoy the kiss, this might be down to lack of experience for both of you. Or you may be too nervous. Allow yourself some room for improvement!

WHEN DISASTER STRIKES

Even if it all goes wrong, don't worry. If you accidentally nip his tongue, bump teeth or dribble, it's not the end of the world. Kissing should be fun, not serious!

TRY THIS Laugh it off and start again. The more you kiss your boyf the better you'll get at it.

SNOG SPOILER *Freaking out, apologising or running off are just lame. And if he's a rubbish kisser, don't tell anyone. Nasty comments will just get you a bad rep.*

The Kiss

You're there. You're millimetres away from his lips. Do not panic. This is what you need to do…

1 Close your eyes. Yes, your crush may be fit, but we bet even Justin Bieber would seem a little bit creepy if you were eyeball-to-eyeball with him. There is such a thing as getting too close.

2 Tilt your head gently to one side. A general rule is, if you're right handed, you'll probably tilt to the right, and vice versa if you're left-handed.

3 Don't fret, freak out or try to second-guess what he'll do next. Take it slowly and stay focused so you'll have plenty of time to react, no matter how he plays it.

4 Start out gently – going straight for a 'tongue-sandwich' is a bit full-on!

5 Remember to breathe through your nose. Passing out mid-kiss may scare him.

6 Relax… then the kiss that you share will come more naturally.

CHAPTER FIVE
BOY-O-RAMA
Get sussed!

10 SIGNS HE'S THE ONE!

How to know when he's for keeps…

1 You get butterflies every time you see him. Your hands go clammy, your heart skips a beat, your face feels warm as a blush spreads over it… Yup, you've got it bad, girl!

2 **He never moans when you choose a chick flick or force him to watch the *Eastenders* omnibus. He's happy to sit through any TV show at all, as long as he's with you.**

3 For some unknown reason, you find his bad habits cute. You don't even get grossed out when he burps the alphabet! Just don't tell him this or he may start to push his luck.

4 **He's never too embarrassed to hold your hand or give you a hug and kiss – not even when he's around his mates or, even worse, his mum's in the room!**

5 You've dragged him round the shops for three hours and made him wait while you've tried on 101 different outfits, but he's still smiling and complimenting you.

6 He's always buying you little pressies. They don't have to be expensive – just your fave sweets or his last Rolo in a fancy box. No special occasion, he does it just because…

7 Even when he's not actually around, just thinking about him is enough to get you grinning away like the Cheshire Cat from *Alice in Wonderland*!

8 When you're together, he can't take his eyes off you. And he always notices when you're wearing a new top or you've just had your hair done.

9 You can imagine yourselves still together and getting on brilliantly well a year from now – maybe even longer. And thinking about it doesn't freak either of you out in the slightest!

10 His fave footie team are playing their most important match of the season, but he's missing it to help out at your little sister's birthday party. Aww…

BOY-O-RAMA

IS IT LOVE OR LUST?

You've met a hot guy, but is it the real thing or just a quick fling? Read our signs to see whether he's a one-week wonder or a long-term prospect...

YOU'VE STOPPED NOTICING OTHER LADS

Sure, the pizza boy's fit, but he's not a patch on your gorgeous boyf. In fact nobody comes close. Truth is since the two of you got together you've completely forgotten that other boys exist. Well almost – you're still human, right?

HE MAKES YOU FEEL GOOD ABOUT YOURSELF

Even when you're having a bad hair day, he still thinks you're beautiful. You might be slopping around in your trackies with the greasiest hair on the planet, but in his eyes you always look your best. That's because he loves the real you!

YOU MISS HIM WHEN YOU'RE NOT TOGETHER

It might sound cheesy, but he's one of your mates as well as your boyfriend, right? if your mate goes on holiday you miss her, and it's the same with your lad, but it's good to spend time away from each other, so you've got more to talk about when you hook up.

HIS GOOD POINTS OUTNUMBER THE BAD

OK, so not everyone is perfect, but love is blind and it's easy to overlook an individual's bad points. Make a list of your lad's pros and cons – if the downside list is longer than your arm it might be time to rethink your relationship. If not, you're onto a good thing.

HE'D NEVER MAKE YOU CHOOSE BETWEEN HIM AND YOUR MATES

Anyone (including your mates) who makes you choose between them and another person is a loser. You should never have to make a choice about who you hang with – that decision is always yours. So if your lad is laid back enough to let you hang with whoever you want, he's a guy worth holding onto.

YOU KNOW YOU CAN TRUST HIM... AND HE TRUSTS YOU

If a relationship is going to work you need to be able to trust this guy with your past as well as your present. Any issues from your history (maybe you fancied his best mate ages ago…) should stay there and not affect your future together. Some things don't need to be discussed. If you trust him and show him that you are trustworthy, too, then the green-eyed monster should stay well and truly hidden!

YOU DON'T WANT TO CHANGE HIM, AND HE HASN'T TRIED TO CHANGE YOU

If the last thing you asked your lad to do was get his hair cut like Becks, just because you've got a crush, then chances are it's not the real deal! Trying to change your guy will never work, and he shouldn't be trying to change you either. Be happy with each other the way you are, or maybe think about finding someone else. Remember, you fell for each other because you were both being you, so don't go changing.

WARNING! TOXIC BOYS ARE BAD FOR YOUR HEALTH!

You crave him like chocolate, even though you know he's the last lad you should be getting into. Why do some boys appeal even more to a gal because of – not despite – the fact they're 100% toxic?

SO, WHAT'S THE APPEAL?

Whether he's a troublemaker who's always in detention or a year 12 with piercings, a lad with a toxic streak is destined to flick your 'weak at the knees' switch. They constantly draw attention to themselves and their popularity and playfulness can be very magnetic. Or maybe it's do with the excitement of knowing that something is bad for us – like too much pizza and cheesecake, or high heeled shoes! Certainly, the idea of dating a toxic lad is thrilling. But it's worth remembering that, at some point, he will let you down. Sadly, bad boys are charming at best, and at worst, unreliable. Each girl he dates thinks she'll be the one to change him – but nobody can, you included. Bad boys are like a fake designer handbag – fabulously perfect seen from a distance, but all frayed lining and wonky stitching up close. Get what we're saying?

TOXIC BOYS COME IN ALL DIFFERENT SHAPES AND SIZES — HERE'S HOW TO SPOT THEM SO YOU CAN KEEP YOURSELF AT A SAFE DISTANCE!

❤ THE 'I'M NOT OVER MY EX YET' BOY

TOXIC TRAIT She ditched him months back yet, every time he opens his mouth, he says, 'Wow, that's great, but my ex did…' Aargh! You deserve a boy who appreciates you for being you and never compares you to his ex. Ever.

❤ THE MUMMY'S BOY

TOXIC TRAIT He's sweet and polite, but acts like there's a mini version of his mum sitting on his shoulder telling him what to do and think. You'll meet her early on, just so he can see if she approves of you. C'mon, if he can't tell for himself how fab you are, kick him to the kerb!

❤ THE 'LAD'S LAD' BOY

TOXIC TRAIT He may seem cute and lovely, but beware. The instant his bezzie calls, he'll blow you out without a second thought. And don't ask to meet his gang – when he sees them, it's strictly boys only. Or if you do get an introduction, he may act like a childish idiot, showing you up to try and impress them.

❤ THE SPORTY BOY

TOXIC TRAIT He's fit and competitive, born to win – but you always come a poor second to his fave sports. Exercise may mean he's buff, but stick around and you'll discover the reality. That he always smells a tad sweaty – gross! – and never shuts up about footie. Yawn…

❤ THE OLDER BOY

TOXIC TRAIT Some girls reckon dating an older lad makes them seem more mature – but he may see you as easier to boss around. He'll act like he knows it all and might try to talk you into dating him behind your parent's back. When they find out, which they will, they'll ground you until you're 18 – and trust us, no lad is worth that!

TOXIC BOY VS MR NICE

Is your crush a goodie or a baddie?

Which of these would attract you to a boy?
A Dark mysterious eyes to stare into
B He's a good listener

The type of lad you normally crush on is...
A Tall, spiky dark hair and a moody scowl
B Clean cut, with floppy blond hair and puppy dog eyes

What would be the best pressie your crush could buy you?
A A skull-and-crossbones ring
B A diamond ring

How intelligent would your ideal boy have to be?
A As long as he knows where all the best parties are, that's good enough for me!
B Quite – I'd like to have nice chats with him

What would be your ideal way to spend time with your crush?
A Crashing a gig and staying out late
B A romantic walk in the park

MOSTLY A'S
You've got it bad for Mr Treat 'Em Mean! While a rough 'n' ready type may seem exciting, ask yourself what's more important – someone you can crash a party with or a boy who'd throw a party for you?

MOSTLY B'S
You're into Mr Sweet 'n' Sensitive! He'll treat you like a princess, buy you flowers and chocs and always ring when he says he will. Nice boys may not live life on the edge, but they'll respect you. We ♥ nice boys!

Bad-for-you boys

So you can't help crushing on Mr. Wrong, huh? Here's how to deal with it.

HE'S: *Your friend's crush*

When you crush on a boy who your bud already likes, it's a dangerous move. Sure, sometimes it feels like you "just can't help it" but you are in control of whether or not you act on a crush. Before you do anything, think about the consequences, like hurting your gal-pal's feelings and your other friends' reactions. Would you be okay with it if the situation was reversed and she was making a play for your guy?

THE VERDICT: This is one of those situations where

loyalty and friendship play a big part. The smart thing to do is to keep your feelings to yourself (or share them with one pal who you know would never, ever blab) and don't act on them. Who knows, maybe your friend will lose interest in this guy and then you'll have your chance. If you decide you have to go for this boy now, you risk losing a friend, so choose carefully.

HE'S: *A dude your parents hate (or would if they knew him)*

Maybe you like a bad boy or your crush is much older than you. Or he's just really different from what your folks are used to. The thing is, your parents' approval of your crush isn't just a bonus. If you really want to date this guy, then their OK is 100% necessary because they still control what you do and who you see. If they dislike this boy, what chance do you have, right?

THE VERDICT: You can
try to reason with your parents. If they're worried he's trouble, reassure them that you'd never let a boy force you into anything you don't think is right. Also remember that your 'rents want the best for you, so they could have a genuine reason to dislike your boy. Think about it, are they right? Maybe your folks despise him because of something superficial, like his hairstyle or the way he dresses? If that's the case, let them get to know him. After they all spend time together, your parents might change their mind about your crush. Still, if they absolutely forbid you to date him, all you can do is accept it and move on.

HE'S: *Hot, but not very nice*

We've all been there, liking a boy who may be cute and funny, but who can also be kinda mean and thoughtless at times. Maybe he never calls when he says he will, or texts you saying how much he digs you, but ignores you in front of his friends. Or, he makes fun of, or picks on others. Still you can't help being attracted to him. Grrr.

THE VERDICT: This boy may be an inconsiderate
loser who doesn't care who he hurts. Or, maybe he's a decent guy who acts like a fool because he's totally immature (and awkward around girls). Whatever his deal is, his actions speak louder than words. The bottom line is, if you like being treated badly and like the drama, go for it. Or (duh) find a sweet boy who knows how to act around a girl and make him the new object of your affection.

HE'S: *The gorgeous boy who doesn't know you're even alive*

This boy is so cool that he makes you drool. You always, always apply lip gloss right before you know you're going to pass him in the corridor between classes, but he's never noticed you. He may be super-cool, but you think he's probably 'out of your league.' It's fun crushing on a guy like that because it's like fantasising about a celeb you get to see everyday. But is it totally pointless?

THE VERDICT: The good
news is this situation is completely open to possibilities. If you want, you can continue to adore him from afar, like showing up at his football match or hoping to catch a glimpse of him in the café. It's kind of stalker-like, but fun. Or, you could actually talk to him, which, of course, involves the possibility of rejection. The final option is to forget about him and set your eyes on a boy who knows you exist. Find a hottie who will appreciate your lip gloss application and your devotion! It's your life, so you call the shots.

IT'S NEVER GOING TO WORK

YOU LIKED HIM, BUT HE DIDN'T ASK YOU OUT AGAIN

This happens to everyone – even the girl all the boys are in love with. Still, all you can think is "What did I do wrong?" Nothing! He just wasn't the one for you. If someone asks, "What's up with you guys?" simply say, "It just didn't work out." Don't trash-talk about him, or people will know that you're the one who got burned. Keeping your cool will help you feel like a girl who's in control. So the next time you see him, act casual – smile and keep walking. After all, you had a life before him – and you still do!

GIVE HIM THE HEAVE-HO

So, he's not the boy for you. One down, 10 million to go! If he calls, say, "I had a nice time, but I don't think we're right for each other." You're not saying anything's wrong with the boy, but things just didn't click between you two. Be honest without being snotty. Someday you may find yourself in his spot, so always remember; karma works!

JUST FRIENDS

Girl/boy friendships can be weird, especially if he's crushing on you or if everyone assumes you two are an item. Things don't have to be awkward. Check out our tips on how solve the most common relationship riddles – plus some essential do's and don'ts from a lad's point of view.

YOU'RE JUST FRIENDS, BUT...

...EVERYONE THINKS
YOU'RE A COUPLE

He's always bringing you sweet surprises. You two sure seem coupled up, so are you really surprised that your friends think you're into each other?

FUTURE FRIEND POTENTIAL:
✷ HIGH

Unfortunately, you can't stop others from gossiping or spreading rumours. At the same time, though, maybe you need to reassess the situation. Their romantic radar might be picking up on something yours isn't. But as long as neither you are harbouring secret sentiments for the other, you've got a good chance of sustaining your friendship for the long run.

BOY ADVICE

DO: Clarify the sitch with your friends if their wisecracks are truly bothering you. Tell them they need to back off a bit because girls and boys can be just pals.

DON'T: Go out of your way to constantly point out you're not a couple. You'll seem less believable by protesting too much, and you run the risk of straining things between you and your boy bud.

...HE LIKE-LIKES YOU
(OR AT LEAST YOU THINK HE DOES).

Fact or rumour, word is you boy bud is crushing on you! It can be a sticky situation when a pal wants to be more than just friends. This could be the start of a real romance or the end of a fab friendship, so weigh your options up carefully before you decide to act.

FUTURE FRIEND POTENTIAL:
✳ MEDIUM TO HIGH

The possibility of maintaining your friendship in this case depends on how you found out about the crush and your reaction to the news. If you heard it from someone else and you don't want to get romantic, play it cool and don't change a thing. If he told you himself and you're not interested, let him down gently and explain that his friendship means too much to you to risk a fallout. Initially, he might act a little awkward, but that shouldn't last. In time hopefully he will move on. If you're also crushing, you should still tread lightly. The consequences of getting involved with a friend can be harsh if things don't work out. Do you want to risk it?

BOY ADVICE

DO: Consider how reliable the info is, especially if you didn't hear it directly from your boy-bud – you know how the telephone game works.

DON'T: Throw yourself at him, but don't play hard to get if you like-like him, too.

...YOU'RE CRUSHING ON HIM.

While absentmindedly taking notes in class, you glance down and notice that the only thing on the page is a giant heart with your lad mate's name smack dab in the middle of it. Realising you have feelings for a friend leaves you with a big decision: Stay silent or fess up? If you want to keep this friendship, are you going to have to set your sights on a different hottie?

FUTURE FRIEND POTENTIAL:
✳ MEDIUM TO HIGH

Right now, the ball's in your court. If you put yourself out there, he might breathe a sigh of relief and reveal that he's into you too – he was just too chicken to tell you. He could also panic and start making excuses not to hang out anymore. Telling him how you feel is a scary move, but if it's really important to you, be brave and speak up!

BOY ADVICE

DO: Write out a pro/con list for telling him how you feel. Then compare the columns to see what's best for you – and be honest!

DON'T: Give in to the temptation to ask friends for advice. You don't need everyone to know the details of who you're crushing on.

...YOU USED TO BE A COUPLE

This one's tricky! You and your former flame may want to do the 'just friends' thing, but being pals with an ex is no easy task. Understand that sooner or later, one of you will probably start dating someone else and that may hurt the person who's still single.

FUTURE FRIEND POTENTIAL:
✷ LOW TO MEDIUM

For this scenario to work, both of you have to want the friendship and play an equal part in building it. A one-sided relationship is bound to fail. Whatever caused the breakup will linger in the back of your minds, but if you communicate well and talk through the problem, your friendship might stand a chance.

BOY ADVICE

DO: Keep the little green monster in check. While jealousy is natural, it can wreak havoc on a budding friendship.

DON'T: Think you're going to be best buds overnight. The wounds of a broken romance take time to heal!

CLINGY CRUSHES

When your dream date holds on a little too tight...

Attentive lads are a good thing, right? Any girl who's spent an evening staring at a silent phone would envy you the 'problem' of being bombarded with texts and calls by a boyfriend. But a clingy crush can quickly become irritating, demanding, even a bit smothering. You like that he likes you, but why can't he give you even a minute to yourself? When your crush turns out to be clingier than Velcro-covered ivy wrapped in clingfilm, how should you deal with him?

 DO TALK TO HIM

Tell him gently that you're feeling overwhelmed by all the attention he's giving you, and explain that you need a bit of space now and again. He's not a mind-reader and he can't stop crowding you unless he's aware he's doing it.

 DO REASSURE HIM

Make sure he knows that, just because you want to spend more time with your mates, it doesn't mean you've stopped fancying him altogether. The more secure he feels within your relationship, the less he'll feel the need to keep hounding you for attention.

 TAKE IT AS A COMPLIMENT

The constant phone calls may be annoying but – admit it – as long as it's not controlling or threatening, all this attention is actually quite flattering. What you see as clinginess is just his way of showing he cares. Why be mad at him for that?

 DO GIVE HIM A CHANCE

If he's only just met or begun to date you, the novelty and excitement may mean he gets carried away. Give it a few weeks and he may become more laid-back about things.

✗ DON'T BE GROUCHY IN THE HOPE HE'LL LEAVE YOU ALONE

If he's seriously clingy, the likelihood is he'll do whatever it takes to make you like him. Picking a fight will only make him grovel in an attempt to make up, which will mean more calls, more texts and more irritation as he gets more desperate.

✗ DON'T LAUGH OR DISS HIM BEHIND HIS BACK

Niceness isn't a crime and slating him for it will transform you into something straight out of *Mean Girls*. If you have a problem with him, talk to him about it directly and be kind and tactful. Don't hurt him any more than you have to.

✗ DON'T USE HIM

Knowing a lad will do anything for you is not an excuse to get him to pay for everything, fetch and carry for you or come and go whenever it suits you. It's a sad way to treat him, not smart.

✗ DON'T EXPECT MIRACLES

You have a right to tell him not to be so clingy, but some lads are a tad full on, and mean no harm by it. If it bugs you that much, maybe you're just not compatible as a couple.

Three's a crowd

If your best mate's got herself a hot new lad, make sure you don't get left out in the cold...

♥ SHE'S ALWAYS ON ABOUT HIM

Each morning she bounds up to you, desperate to share the details of their latest date. But if she tells you just one more time how fab he is, you're going to scream, be sick – or both!

WHAT TO DO

When you get something new – like shoes, an ipod or, yes, a lad – it's natural to want to show them off at first. Indulge her for a bit, but if she won't let up, joke about her being obsessed or change the subject when she mentions him. But try not to fall out over him – she still needs her gal-pals, even if she doesn't realise it at the mo!

HOW SHE'S FEELING

She's so into him, she's beyond understanding why you might not want to talk about him all the time. Make it clear you're happy for her – you don't want her thinking that you're jealous – but remind her there are other things in life, too, like mates, school and even your own crushes!

♥ HE'S NOT RIGHT FOR HER

You've heard things about this lad, like he's got a rep as a user. You don't want your best mate getting hurt, but you don't want to seem like you're bad-mouthing him or interfering, either.

WHAT TO DO

Is he actually as bad as people say? Get your facts right. Did he really two-time anyone? Or if he dumped a girl, was it for a good reason? It may be an ex spreading mean lies to get revenge. If it does sound like he's trouble, tell your mate what you know, but don't make a drama of it. Then let her make her own decisions about him.

HOW SHE'S FEELING

He'll be with her forever — er, won't he? All the rumours may be scaring her and, if you add to them without being able to back up what you're saying she'll feel betrayed. If she decides to give him a chance, that's her call — just be there for her if she needs you.

♥ I FEEL LIKE A SPARE PART

Your pal has asked you to hers for the first girls' night in you've had since she started dating her boyfriend. It's just like old times, then the doorbell rings. Yep, it's him – he was "just passing by and thought he'd drop in to say hi". All fine, except two hours later, he's still there. They snuggle up on the sofa, making you feel awkward. Then, while you're in the middle of talking, he starts to snog her. So much for your girlie night in – it's like you're not even there! Humph.

WHAT TO DO

First, tell her you think he's cool and that you appreciate how much she's into him. Then say you miss hanging out with her. Suggest that maybe a bit of girlie time away from him would do them both good – they wouldn't want to end up feeling like they're living in each other's pockets.

HOW SHE'S FEELING

She probably knows full well that she's neglecting you a bit, and chances are she even feels guilty about it. But she may also think you're such a good friend that you don't have any problem with him being around. If you do, then tell her, but be tactful and don't try to make her choose between the two of you.

💜 I NEVER SEE HER!

You used to do everything together. She'd phone you straight after every episode of 'Enders, pair up with you for that tricky school project and help you to pick that perfect outfit at the shops. So now where is she when you need her? Er, with him, that's where!

WHAT TO DO

Don't mope in front of the TV night after night. Why put your life on hold in the hope that she'll see sense and get in touch? Hang out with your other mates, or even make new ones – try joining a sports or hobby club in your area. And tell your mate you'd like to see a bit more of her or how much fun you're having – it may jolt her into realising how wrapped up she's been in her lad.

HOW SHE'S FEELING

She's seen him every night this week – fab or what? But it'll soon dawn on her that maybe he doesn't want to talk about period pains, boy bands or nail varnish. And how long before she admits to herself that watching his TV choices bores her? Bet she's dialling your number before you know it. When she does, be nice. You may be tempted to be a bit offish, just to give her a taste of how you felt, but remember, you want your mate back!

BOY BEZZIES

So your NBF is male? Well, congrats – every girl needs at least one great lad mate! Here's how to make the most of it – and how to avoid the classic pitfalls, too!

THE GOOD

SLOB OUT!

This is one of the best things about hanging out with a lad mate. Boy pals take no notice of what you wear, so grab your comfiest trackie – yup, those 1,000-times-washed, greying, tatty ones – chuck on a tee three sizes too big and you're good to go!

BLUNT TALK

There's no pretence with boys, they're rubbish liars by nature so they'll always speak with total, often brutal, honesty. Girl mates will say what you want to hear like "Your crush fancies you, but he's shy." A lad will say, "You're just not his type." Tactless, but 100% reliable – he won't raise any false hopes just to make you happy.

AGONY UNCLE

As a boy himself, your lad mate is brimming with insider advice on how to handle the dating minefield. He knows it all – from tactics to get a hottie talking to how long you should wait to text after a first date. Having an expert guide to the confusing male brain puts you at such a big advantage it almost feels unfair on your crushes!

THE BAD

BECOMING BOY-LIKE

Don't take on too many laddish traits. Stay true to your girlie ways and make sure you hang out with your gal pals, too! It's one thing to slob out at the weekend, but when you start debating new rugby laws and how old-school stunts were so much better than CGI effects, you know you've gone too far.

FILM FEUDS

He wants to watch an action movie and you want to watch a rom-com. He points out that his movie is jam-packed with gruesome vampire action. You agree and say that's why you should watch your film. He storms out muttering something about the lameness of girls. Prepare for many battles like this.

HOUSE TRAINED

As in, boys are so not! They think breaking wind is hilarious. They sniff their armpit and decide having a shower can wait until tomorrow. They leave stinking socks, uneaten food and half –drunk cups of tea lying around to fester, like they're conducting a scientific experiment. Aside from the odd panic over deorant when he meets a girl he fancies, he's not going to change – and, the sooner you accept this, the better. Whatever you do, don't nag him like his mum or the invites to hang out will start to slide…

Ask Lisa!

Need some advice on boys? *Mizz* life coach Lisa Clark has the answers...

READY TO DATE?

I've never had a boyfriend or even kissed a boy. I think I want one, but I'm so nervous around them, the thought of a date makes my stomach hurt.

You can't and shouldn't force yourself to be ready for a boyfriend. It's best to wait until everything feels right. That might not be the answer you want to hear, but it will happen naturally. In the meantime, concentrate on being friends with the boys you know. Remember, they probably have some of the same dating fears as you do.

YO-YO DATING

I have a boyfriend right now and things are okay except that we keep breaking up and getting back together. I get so jealous when he hangs around with other girls, and when we aren't a couple, he seems to talk to me more than when we're together. What's going on?

Who's the one doing the break up? If it's your boyfriend, then maybe he's trying to tell you he likes you, but isn't ready to get serious. If it's you, ask yourself why seeing him around other girls makes you second-guess your decision. It's tough to admit a relationship isn't working, but sometimes making a clean break – and then keeping your distance – helps you get over it faster.

STUCK IN THE MIDDLE

My friend's boyfriend tried to kiss me and my friend saw! Instead of yelling at her boyfriend, I ended up with the blame. I don't know how to make things better between us.

Deep down, your pal probably knows the truth, but isn't ready to face up to the fact that her boyfriend is a loser. She's most likely humiliated, but doesn't want to break up with her boyf. Get together with your bud and explain your side of the story. If she's not willing to believe you, then you've got to ask yourself if she's really that good of a friend. And, if he's that much of a loser, she'll realise it soon enough.

SINGLE-MINDED?

I'm 14 years old and I've never had a boyfriend. A couple of guys have asked me out, but I said no because I didn't think I liked them. After I turned them down, though, I realised I really do like them. What should I do?

You might think you really like a boy once the opportunity to date him has passed, but trust your instinct that told you otherwise. Having a boyfriend for the first time can be a little scary, and you might not be ready to take the plunge just yet. When you truly crush on a boy, you'll know.

BASHFUL AROUND BOYS

Sometimes I have trouble talking to boys. I don't know what to say and get embarrassed easily. Can you give me some pointers?

One of the easiest ways to get over boy fright is to remember that they are as nervous and as unsure of themselves as you are! If you concentrate on putting them at ease by asking questions that require more than a 'yes' or 'no' answer and giving lots of smiles – you'll relax and make a great impression.

BOYFRIEND OR BEST FRIEND?

My best male friend and I are really close, but he doesn't know that I secretly like him. Should I tell him, or should we just stay friends?

If you come right out and tell your boy pal you like him and he doesn't feel the same way, it could end your friendship. Try to find out a more subtle way to gauge his feelings. Casually ask him what kind of girl he wants to date. Then give him a chance to show he likes you, too. If he doesn't, be prepared to swallow your pride and keep him as a close bud.

WRITE OR WRONG

I've been crushing on one boy since year 5. When I talk to him, it's usually about maths or science. Do you you think I should write him a letter telling him how I feel?

A letter is a great way to get your feelings out, but seeing all those emotions on paper might be just a little bit overwhelming to a boy, especially one who's more comfortable with equations and formulas. Don't rush your crush. Instead, ask him to hang out with you and your pals or go to a movie together. Get to know each other in a more social setting And make sure to talk about things other than schoolwork!

MOVING ON

I've been going out with my boyfriend for a while now, but I'm not sure about my feelings for him anymore. Maybe I should break up with him? I don't know what to do.

The fact that you're questioning your feelings for this guy

m **BOY-O-RAMA**

means you're not ready to commit to him long term. Tell him things are too serious for you and you want to take a break. That breathing room should give you the time and space to figure out how you really feel about him.

VANISHING ACT

I met a guy on holiday and thought we really clicked. After coming home, though, I never heard from him.

Before you jump to the conclusion he wasn't crushing on you, think of all the other possible reasons behind his silence: He lost your number or email address, for instance. Or maybe he's not sure how you feel and doesn't want to get rejected. Give him the benefit of the doubt and contact him. Tell him you just wanted to say hi, then see how he responds. If he's thrilled to hear from you – hooray! If not, at least you'll know for sure and you can move on.

BOYS ARE OKAY, BUT BEING SINGLE ROCKS BECAUSE...

 You can watch your favourite chick flick in peace. That's right, no whines and grumbles from a boy-shape and you don't have to share your chocolate stash either – hurrah!

 You can drool over the Robert Pattinson clone in your maths class (and the cutie in science too) all you want without so much as ounce of guilt.

 No checking your mobile every 30 seconds, wondering why he hasn't texted back.

 Lip-gloss always stays on longer when you're living a smooch-free life.

 When a school disco rolls around, you can boldly ask whoever you like. Or, dance the night away with your besties!

 No more boring football convos. (Unless you're a fan, obviously.)

 It's just one less thing you have to fight about with your parents.

 You don't have to hang with his friends, meet his folks or make any other social adjustments, instead you get to hang out with your gal-pals as often as possible – fab!

 No BF means no icky break up followed by days of tears and tubs of ice cream.

 You can be all about Y-O-U, which in turn will make you a better girlfriend when a good guy does come knocking at your door.

Write your boy notes here

....
....
....
....
....
....
....
....
....
....
....
....
....
....
....
....
....
....
....
....
....

Write your boy notes here

....
....
....
....
....
....
....
....
....
....
....
....
....
....
....
....
....
....
....
....
....
....
....

Write your boy notes here

....

....

....

....

....

....

....

....

....

....

....

....

....

....

....

....

....

....

....

....

....

Write your boy notes here

....
....
....
....
....
....
....
....
....
....
....
....
....
....
....
....
....
....
....
....

Write your boy notes here

....
....
....
....
....
....
....
....
....
....
....
....
....
....
....
....
....
....
....

Write your boy notes here

....
....
....
....
....
....
....
....
....
....
....
....
....
....
....
....
....
....
....
....
....

Write your boy notes here

Write your boy notes here